UNIQUE ADAPTATIONS OF
Nighttime Animals

by Tracey Hecht

FABLED FILMS PRESS
NEW YORK CITY

info@fabledfilms.com

Published by Fabled Films LLC, New York

ISBN: 978-1-944020-72-9

Library of Congress Control Number: 2021953346

First Edition: October 2022

1 3 5 7 9 10 8 6 4 2

Book produced by WonderLab Group
Science writing by Emma Carlson Berne
Designed by Project Design Company
Photo edited by Annette Kiesow
Educational review by Lauren Woodrow
Copyedited by Lori Merritt
Proofread by Molly Reid
Indexed by Connie Binder
Character illustrations by Kate Liebman
Typeset in Stemple Garamond, Mrs. Ant, Pacific Northwest Rough Letters, and Filson Soft
Printed by Everbest in China

FABLED FILMS PRESS

NEW YORK CITY

fabledfilms.com

For information on bulk purchases for promotional use please contact Fabled Films Press Sales department at info@fabledfilms.com

NOTE TO READERS

Throughout the book, you will see important ***vocabulary words in bold italic type.*** You can find the meaning of these words in the Word Glossary on **page 120.**

The Nocturnals Explore
Unique Adaptations of
Nighttime Animals

TABLE OF CONTENTS

Saltwater Crocodile

Go exploring
with
The Nocturnals

Dawn raised her head, sniffing the fresh night air. In the sky, a full moon was rising. "Bismark? Tobin?" the red fox called out to her friends.

Bismark scampered down a nearby tree trunk. "Good evening, Dawn!" the sugar glider hollered. "I see by the moon that it is time for adventure!"

"Did someone say adventure?" Tobin asked as he emerged from the brush. The sleepy pangolin blinked his little eyes and smoothed the scales on his tail.

"I thought we'd meet some new friends," Dawn said, sitting down and coiling her tail neatly around her paws. "Bandicoots, aye-ayes, tuataras, and jerboas. These are some of the animals we're going to meet. They're fascinating. And they're all nocturnal."

"Bandicoots and tuataras?" Bismark exclaimed. "Sounds like adventure to me!" Bismark jumped up onto Dawn's back. "Let's go!"

Tobin giggled.

"Off we go," Dawn agreed. And the three nocturnal friends ventured into the night.

INTRODUCTION: DISCOVER ANIMALS AT NIGHT

Animals that are active at night are known as *nocturnal* animals. The nighttime life has a lot of advantages for these incredible creatures. The temperature is cooler, which is good for animals who live in hot *climates* like the desert. Small animals can hide more easily from *predators* in the dark. And predators don't have to compete with daytime animals for *prey*. They get the hunting all to themselves. To navigate the dark, many of these animals have developed special *adaptations* to help them survive and thrive.

Red Fox

Sugar Glider

Cape Pangolin

Day to Night

So what about animals that get up with the sun? Any animals that are awake during the day and sleep at night are *diurnal*. Humans and millions of other animals, like songbirds, chimpanzees, and elephants, are diurnal. Others, like coyotes and foxes, live in the in-between. These animals are *crepuscular*, and they are active in the low light of dawn and dusk. They are able to avoid predators in the semi-dark. Another group of animals are *cathemeral*. Their waking and sleeping patterns are a bit more irregular. They are sometimes active during the day and sometimes at night.

NOCTURNAL ANIMAL FEATURES

Nocturnal animals have special features that help them survive in the dark. As you explore the animals in this book, look out for these icons that will tell you about their special adaptations and other important info:

EYES
These nocturnal animals have big eyes and big pupils to let the maximum amount of light in.

EARS
Some nocturnal creatures have especially large ears. If they can't see super well in the dark, they can hear instead.

NOSE
Many nocturnal animals have sensitive noses and whiskers for sniffing out plants and insects. There's no need for sunlight when you can just smell your dinner.

EXPERT HIDER
To protect themselves from predators, some nocturnal animals hide during the day or use camouflage.

INTO THE LIGHT
Most nocturnal animals only come out at night. However, a few will sometimes venture out during the day or the semi-dark hours of dusk and dawn.

ENDANGERED
Some nocturnal animals are safe in the wild, though look out for this icon, which means the nocturnal animal is in trouble.

Night Notes

As you read, find the flashlight to learn even more about an animal's special nocturnal features!

"First stop is Australia," Dawn called as she padded through a wide, grassy area. "I feel so at home here."

"Um, Dawn, aren't we in suburbia?" Tobin asked.

"Why yes! I think this is someone's front lawn," Bismark exclaimed.

Dawn smiled. "Well, whether in an open field or a perfectly manicured lawn, we foxes can call each home."

Red Fox

Chapter 1

FOXES EVERYWHERE

Known for their smarts, red foxes have adapted to live in many different habitats throughout the world, including in North America, Europe, Australia, and northern Africa. Foxes thrive in forests and on grasslands and even on cold mountaintops and in blazing hot deserts. They can also live in cities. You may have even seen a fox in your backyard!

FUN FACT
Red foxes store food in underground *caches* and come back to them later when they are hungry.

Foxes often make their homes in the edges of yards or neighborhoods, where there is some natural cover like bushes or trees. This puts them right near people—and their tasty garbage cans.

Tricky Hunters

Like their coyote, wolf, and dog relatives, foxes are good swimmers and fast runners. They can sprint up to 30 miles an hour (48 km/h) after their dinner. Their speed combined with their sharp eyesight and good sense of smell helps them find food in the dark. These tricky hunters aren't picky eaters. They eat a range of small animals, from rabbits and frogs to fruit, worms, and fish!

Red foxes get pretty jumpy while on the hunt. They may leap up to six feet (2 km) in the air and then pounce on their meal with their front paws. This move helps them capture and hold their prey quickly before it can escape. Hunting foxes will stand still, listen for the unlucky rodent, and then furiously dig into the earth to find it.

DID YOU KNOW?
The fennec fox has huge ears that help release heat during the hot days in its desert habitat.

Night Notes

Red foxes are nocturnal; however, they are sometimes active during dusk, dawn, and even daylight hours. At night, they locate their prey using their amazing sense of hearing. They have such good ears that they can hear rodents moving around underground!

Red or Gray?

Red foxes can be confused with gray foxes. Despite their names, gray foxes can have some red fur and red foxes can have some gray fur. So how can you tell it's a red fox? Look at the tail! Red foxes have white tips, and gray foxes have black tips.

Tail Talk

Red foxes are also known for their long, bushy tails. They use their tails both as a nose cover in cold weather and to "talk" to other foxes. A tail sticking up means either "We're play-fighting!" or "We're for-real-fighting!" A U-shaped tail means "Let's have a game together!" A puffed-up tail means "Watch out! Danger is near!"

Our high-pitched bark is sometimes confused with an owl hooting—especially at night.

Playtime

Play-Fighting

Watch Out!

CARING FOR KITS
Both mother and father foxes take turns leaving the den and hunting for food to bring back to their babies, called kits.

Fox Babies

When it's time to have babies, foxes will line their burrows with dried grass to make a cozy nest. About a month after her babies are born, the mother fox begins feeding them regurgitated food—that's food that she eats and then chokes up! Eventually, fox parents will bring back live rodents so the babies can practice hunting them.

Threats to Foxes

Most of the time, red foxes are the ones doing the eating, yet they do have some predators. Eagles and coyotes will snatch fox babies and young foxes who have just left their dens. Bears, wolves, or mountain lions might attack adult red foxes. But most threats to foxes include getting sick from disease. These canines are also still sometimes trapped for their fur and tails. Or people target them because they are seen as pests.

FUN FACT
Many backyard foxes make their dens underneath porches, where there are often lots of tasty rodents!

FOXES ON THE HUNT

Scientists have known for a long time that birds, turtles, dung beetles, sharks, bees, and other animals use Earth's magnetic field to navigate.

The magnetic field is a natural force that creates energy deep within our planet. This energy pulls differently depending where you are positioned on Earth. Humans can't feel Earth's magnetic field, but some animals can. They use it to orient themselves—almost like they're using an internal GPS.

Scientists have found that foxes actually use Earth's magnetic field to hunt. When it locates an unsuspecting rodent, the fox uses

its internal compass
to judge the distance
and direction between it and
its prey. Foxes, scientists believe,
see a ring of shadow on their eyes. This ring is
always fixed north. So a fox lines the shadow
up with the prey—and then it pounces!

Fox eye calculating prey position

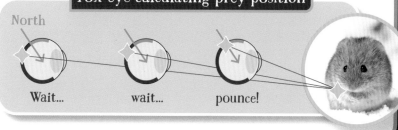

North

Wait...   wait...   pounce!

Once in China, Dawn spotted something and waved to Tobin and Bismark. "Do you see that animal covered with scales?"

"Wait a minute…" Tobin said, twisting to look at his own side.

Bismark thrust his paw in the air. "Let me guess what it is! Is it an iguana?"

Tobin laughed. "It's not an iguana. It's a pangolin. Like me!"

Tree Pangolin

Chapter 2

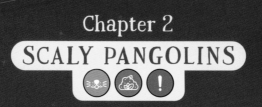

SCALY PANGOLINS

While pangolins might look like scaly lizards, these cute creatures are actually mammals. There are eight *species* of pangolin that live in either Africa or Asia. Though each species is different, all of them are known for a signature feature: their special scales.

FUN FACT
Pangolin scales are made of *keratin*—the same stuff as human fingernails!

Animals covered with scales may seem fearsome and bold; however, pangolins are just the opposite. These gentle anteaters prefer to hide. When afraid, pangolins will roll themselves into a scaly ball! This ball helps shield them from hungry predators.

Hungry for Bugs

Pangolins are master insect eaters—one pangolin can vacuum up around 70 million insects a year! They mainly dine on ants and termites but can eat earthworms and various kinds of larvae, flies, and crickets.

Indian Pangolin

THE NOCTURNALS

Although nocturnal, pangolins aren't very good at seeing in the dark. However, they're great smellers. They sniff along the ground with their sensitive noses, and when they find an ant or termite nest, they dig into it with their front claws. Then, they use their long, sticky tongues to lap up the insects.

Night Notes

Nocturnal pangolins are so shy that scientists have a hard time studying them. During the day, some pangolins sleep in trees or hollow logs, while others dig huge underground burrows—big enough for adult humans to curl up in!

People are learning more about pangolins all the time. Recently, scientists finally figured out that we won't eat insect species we don't recognize. I always make sure I know what I eat!

Dynamic Diggers

Pangolins use their entire bodies to help them dig their sleeping and nesting place. They shovel out the dirt with their powerful front claws and then roll and push themselves against the tunnel walls to mold the dirt. In the winter, they dig their burrows near termite nests so they can easily get to their food, even in the snow and ice. Rubbing against the dirt walls also helps pangolins keep their scales sharp. Perfect protection!

DID YOU KNOW?
Pangolins can close off their nostrils and ear holes while they are eating so attacking ants and termites can't climb in.

Cape Pangolin

TONGUES!
Pangolin tongues are even longer than their bodies.

Tree Pangolin

Baby Pangolins

Pangolins give birth to just one baby at a time. These little pangolins are called pangopups. The mother carries her baby on her tail—except when predators are close and she curls herself up around her pup to protect it.

PROTECTING PANGOLINS

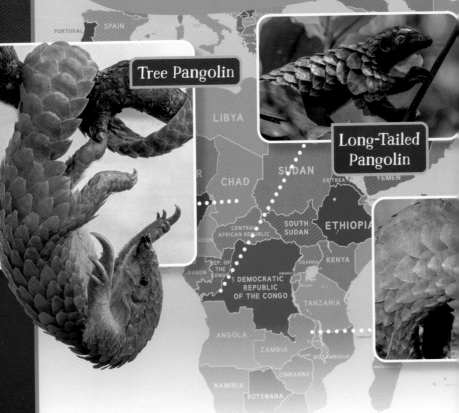

Tree Pangolin

Long-Tailed Pangolin

Pangolins live in Asia and Africa. They make their homes in forests, grasslands, and shrubby bushlands—pretty much anywhere with lots of ants to eat.

Ants are no match for pangolins, but humans are. These endangered creatures are one of the most trafficked animals in the world. This means they are illegally captured or traded. Some people hunt them for their

Indian Pangolin

Chinese Pangolin

Cape Pangolin

Sunda Pangolin

scales, which are used as ingredients in traditional medicines.

Poachers aren't the only danger to pangolins. As land is cleared for farming or building, especially in parts of Asia, pangolins lose the trees, burrows, and insect nests they depend on. In fact, so many pangolins are under threat that all eight species are at risk of extinction and are protected by law.

The Nocturnals landed in the leafy Australian bush. "Trees!" Bismark shouted and leapt toward the nearest trunk. "Home sweet home!"

"Oh!" Tobin exclaimed. "Bismark, can you go up there?"

Bismark scampered up the trunk and disappeared into the leafy treetop. "Fabulous!" he shouted down from the branches. "I already feel better!"

Sugar Glider

Chapter 3
GLIDE, SUGAR GLIDER!

Sugar gliders are about the size of a human hand. Like possums and kangaroos, they're marsupials, which means females have a pouch to carry their babies. They spend their whole lives in the trees. In fact, their furry feet almost never touch the ground!

FUN FACT
Sugar gliders use their muscular tails to carry leaves to their nests.

Fantastic Fliers

While it may look like they're flying from treetop to treetop, sugar gliders don't actually fly. Instead, they glide by using a web of skin that stretches between their back and front limbs. They steer with their outstretched front and back paws and use their furry tails to maintain balance. Their loose skin also acts like a parachute to help them land gently on the branch they're aiming for. A sugar glider can cover more than 150 feet (46 m) in one leap—that's about half the length of a football field!

THE NOCTURNALS

Did you know I have a special grooming comb on my back feet? Two of my toes are fused together. I comb my fur with them!

Night Notes

Sugar gliders' giant eyes are incredibly cute, but they're also important. These aerial acrobats spend their nights jumping from treetop to treetop in the Australian bush and need extra-sharp vision. Their huge eyes let in as much light as possible as they navigate in the moonlight.

QUICK MEAL
Sugar gliders can nab insects in midair with a well-timed leap!

Sweet Treats

High up in the treetops, sugar gliders dine on tree sap and flower pollen. They pluck and eat fruit, too. Sugar gliders don't just eat fruits and plants, though. Using their large, sensitive ears and big eyes, sugar gliders hunt insects like beetles and spiders that crawl along tree trunks and branches. Because they eat both plants and animals, sugar gliders are classified by scientists as *omnivores*.

Bringing Up Baby

Sugar gliders build snuggly nests in the hollows of trees high above the ground. They pile in during the day in groups of 10 and cuddle up to sleep. Female sugar gliders have about one or two babies a year. The babies ride in their mother's pouch, nursing and growing. Mother sugar gliders even customize their babies' food. In the pouch, a mother sugar glider can make special milk for the newborn and different milk for the older baby.

FUN FACT
When baby sugar gliders, called joeys, get too large for mom's pouch, sometimes they'll ride on her back instead.

Getting Cozy

In the winter, life for sugar gliders slows way down. Sometimes, they'll go into a state of hibernation called torpor to conserve energy. In this state, their body temperature falls, they stay very still, and they might even look unconscious. Torpor is temporary, and sugar gliders will stay in it for weeks or months until the weather warms up. Then, it's rise and shine!

FUN FACT
Sugar gliders can make all kinds of noises: hisses, barks, screams, and buzzes. They can even purr like a cat!

DID YOU KNOW?
When a sugar glider feels threatened by an owl or a snake, it might stand up on its hind legs and lift its head to make itself look bigger.

No Pets, Please

Some people keep sugar gliders as pets. However, sugar gliders need lots of space to jump and fly, and they will only eat certain foods. They are also social creatures and need to be with other sugar gliders. So leave them where they belong—in the wild.

MORE GREAT GLIDERS

Sugar gliders aren't the only natural gliders in the animal world. Other species that are active both during the day and at night can also propel themselves through the air without wings:

Parachute Frog

A Wallace's flying frog, also called the parachute frog, launches itself out of trees and spreads out the webbing between its toes to catch the air. Loose skin on its sides also helps this green glider cruise up to 50 feet (15 m) between tree branches. This frog rarely glides to the ground—only to mate and lay eggs.

Wallace's Flying Frog

Paradise Tree Snake

Paradise Tree Snake

Active during the day, a paradise tree snake flings itself out of a tree and glides by flattening out its body in midair. The snake holds itself in a stiff S shape and can even steer by tilting right and left.

Flying Fish

Nocturnal flying fish build up speed in the water by beating their fins furiously. They propel themselves upward, break the water's surface, and stretch out their winglike side fins in the air to keep airborne. A flying fish can glide up to 650 feet (198 m)— almost as long as four Olympic-size swimming pools!

Flying Fish

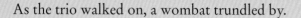

As the trio walked on, a wombat trundled by.

"It's marsupial madness over here!" Bismark exclaimed.

"Oh, wow," Tobin remarked. "And those marsupial pouches are so unique."

Chapter 4

TOUGH WOMBATS

Wombats might look like they're clumsy teddy bears waddling about, but these Australian marsupials can sprint—up to 25 miles an hour (40 km/h) if they have to! Most of the time, wombats aren't sprinting anywhere. They're snuffling through forests and grasslands, marking off their personal eating areas with their scent. These scent lines are a wombat's broadcast system: "Paws off, everyone! This spot's mine!"

Strong Bottoms

Wombats are great diggers, and while they're working away, they have a pretty amazing natural defense—extremely tough bottoms! Their rears are heavily armored with plates of bone, cartilage, fat, skin, and fur. If a predator tries to attack, a wombat can dive into its burrow and plug up the opening with its own rear! Scratching and even biting doesn't hurt its tough tushy.

FUN FACT
Unlike kangaroo pouches, a mother wombat's pouch faces backward, with the opening toward her hind legs.

Common Wombat

Super Snackers

In addition to grass, wombats like to snack on moss, mushrooms, and other fungi. They can't just eat soft foods, though—wombats also need to eat the tough parts of trees and shrubs to wear down their ever-growing front teeth. When they find something particularly good to eat, they guard it from other wombats by screeching and snorting.

No Water Wasted

Desert climate? No problem for wombats! This is because marsupials are fantastic

DID YOU KNOW?
Wombat burrows are so deep, wombats can safely hide in them during wildfires and be protected.

Southern Hairy-Nosed Wombat

THE NOCTURNALS

water-savers. They don't need to drink much to stay hydrated. In fact, wombats get almost all of the water they need just from eating grass! Wombats are also great at keeping the water in their bodies. Then after about a two-and-a-half-week digestion period, a wombat's meal comes out the other end incredibly dry compared to other animals.

We wombats have cube-shaped poop. Some species can poop up to one hundred times a day!

An animal the size of a rabbit wandered past the Brigade.

"Hmm," Bismark said. "Small mammal, check. Marsupial, check. Not a wombat, check."

Dawn and Tobin thought. Then, Tobin sat up. "Oh, I've got it! It's a bandicoot!"

Dawn smiled. "Yes, Tobin. Indeed it is."

Chapter 5

BANDICOOT HIDE-AND-SEEK

Ever heard of a "snout poke"? Just hang around with a bandicoot and you'll find out what it is. This Australian marsupial is, on average, about the size of a rabbit. It has a long, piglike snout and strong, curved front paws. These features—and an excellent sense of smell—are perfect for sniffing out food: fungi, roots, berries, insects, and more. In fact, bandicoots will eat just about anything!

Southern Brown Bandicoot

FUN FACT
Bandicoots mainly live alone and will defend their territories against other bandicoots.

Snout Pokes

As the bandicoot sniffs and pokes its way across the ground, it leaves behind small holes and mounds—snout pokes! And snout pokes bring air into the soil and scatter seeds around, which is useful for the ecosystem.

I found out that the word "bandicoot" comes from a word which means "pigrat." I guess that makes sense: We have snouts like pigs and bodies shaped like rats!

Life in the Pouch

Bandicoot babies are tiny. They're only around one centimeter long when they are born—smaller than a jelly bean!

Baby bandicoots crawl down a cord that leads from their mom's womb to the pouch. Like other digging marsupials, the mother bandicoot's pouch opens at the back, facing her hind legs. This way, she won't accidentally kick dirt into her pouch while searching for food or digging a burrow.

WATERPROOF NESTS
Bandicoots waterproof their nests by covering them with a layer of dirt to keep out the rain.

Night Notes
Coming out at night helps bandicoots evade their predators. Owls and dingoes will eat these small marsupials, though their biggest animal foes are foxes and feral cats and dogs.

DID YOU KNOW?
Bandicoots have joined back toes that they use as a comb to remove ticks.

Speak Up!

Bandicoots don't mind speaking their mind. In fact, these snufflers are quite noisy. Bandicoots will grunt while they're searching for food and make a huffing noise when annoyed by another bandicoot. If in pain, they let out a loud squeal. And when in danger or feeling threatened, bandicoots squeak and whistle. While searching for another bandicoot, they can even tweet and chirp like birds!

Bandicoots in Trouble

Some species of bandicoot are in trouble. As humans have built houses and roads through the Australian bush, bandicoots have lost their habitats. People have tried to trap bandicoots, too, since they sometimes dig up gardens or fields. Some bandicoot populations are now endangered, though governments are trying to help. Certain species of bandicoot are now protected by law.

A MARSUPIAL'S JOURNEY

Brushtail Possum

Australia has a lot of pouched animals. There you'll find the bandicoot, sugar glider, woylie, kangaroo, wallaby, quokka, wombat, Tasmanian devil, and more—this is just a partial list.

WHAT MAKES A MARSUPIAL?

- Marsupials are a type of mammal.
- Females have a belly pouch to nurse and carry babies. A few marsupial species have a fold of skin rather than a pouch.
- Babies are not fully developed when born. They finish growing in their mother's pouch.
- Marsupials have an extra bone to support the pouch.

Rock Wallaby

AUSTRALIA

Koala

How did so many animals with pouches wind up in Australia? Well, scientists believe that marsupials did not evolve there. That's strange for a country that is also an island! Scientists think the oldest marsupials came onto the scene in North America and likely journeyed to South America.

During this time period, about 40 million years ago, South America was connected to Antarctica, which was connected to Australia! Marsupial species traveled over land and when Australia split away from the other continents, they went along for the ride.

Suddenly, Dawn squinted. "Is that a little tiny kangaroo digging away over there?"

"No, it's a woylie on the job!" Bismark squeaked.

Chapter 6

WOYLIES AT WORK

Need some work done in your yard? Just ask a woylie! These furry, guinea pig-size marsupials have a very important job while roaming the forests and grasslands of Australia. Woylies are constantly digging and poking at the soil with their paws as they sniff out the underground fungi they love to eat.

Busy Diggers

Woylies overturn dirt like they're using a garden hoe. Their digging brings water, nutrients, and air into the soil and also spreads around spores and seeds from fungi and plants. All of this activity helps plants grow and nourishes the ecosystem.

FUN FACT
Woylies don't need to drink water! They get all the moisture they need from the fungi they dig up.

Woylie

Helpful Tail

A woylie has a muscular tail that it can use almost like a fifth paw. This *prehensile* tail is strong and flexible. The tail is so strong and handy that scientists sometimes call it a "fifth limb."

Taking Care of Baby

Woylies usually have just one baby at a time. The newborn crawls into its mother's pouch

DID YOU KNOW?
Woylie moms use their tails to help carry grass and other bedding to their nests, where they raise their babies.

and nurses there for about three months. Then, it leaves the pouch just in time for the next newborn to take its place.

Woylies in Danger

These lovable leapers need human help. Foxes and feral cats are predators of woylies, and humans are moving into woylie territory. Woylies are now endangered in the wild. Luckily, Australian animal sanctuaries work hard to protect these marsupials.

Night Notes

Woylies make sure no one can find them while they're sleeping during the day. Using grass and shredded bark, they build dome-shaped nests that are almost impossible to find!

We woylies wrap our tails around our necks to keep warm when we're sleeping.

Tobin scurried under a tree. "Oh goodness! What was that?"

"Calm, calm, my scaly friend," Bismark told him. "Just a powerful owl—quite a large one though—eek!"

Chapter 7

SUPER-SENSING OWLS

Perching high in a tree, the powerful owl—the largest owl in Australia—watches and listens for its dinner. Then, it swoops and pounces!

All over the world, owls rule the nighttime. These birds can be tiny or giant, but they're all raptors. This means they are birds of prey and dine on insects and animals rather than seeds or plants.

Powerful owls mostly dine on possums, though they're big enough to catch the flying fox, the world's biggest bat. These birds perch on tree branches to sleep during the day. This is called roosting, and they like to do it with a snack. They often hold the previous night's kill in their talons until they're ready to eat it.

FUN FACT

Owls have a toe that can rotate forward or backward. This feature helps them clutch branches and grasp prey.

Powerful Owl

I can camouflage myself by lifting up the tufts of feathers on top of my head. This way, the feathers look like leaves or twigs. Handy for all my time in the trees!

Family Birds

When it's time to lay eggs, the male owl builds a nest in a large hollow in an old tree. The female sits on the eggs and takes care of them. Once they hatch, the baby owls stay safe up in the trees with their parents. When the little owls are tired, they hold tight on the branches with their talons, lie on their stomachs, and then turn their heads to the side for a nap!

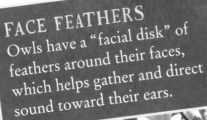

FACE FEATHERS
Owls have a "facial disk" of feathers around their faces, which helps gather and direct sound toward their ears.

Powerful Owls

Night Notes

Owls are nature's nocturnal masters. Their giant eyes let in as much light as possible, which is good for dark nights. With their amazing hearing, owls can hear a rodent moving under layers of snow and ice.

BIRD'S-EYE VIEW

Imagine a human with softball-size eyes that don't move—a scary sight or the perfect night vision adaptation? Owls have huge eyes in the front of their heads. Other raptors, such as eagles and hawks, have eyes on the sides of their heads.

Like many nocturnal animals, owls have a layer of tissue at the back of their eyes that reflects light. This tissue basically gives owls night vision goggles.

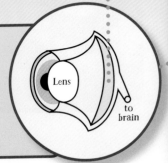

An owl's eyes are not round. Instead, they are tubes that are fixed in the owl's head. These "eye binoculars" help the owl better see its prey.

Lens

to brain

Owls have excellent depth perception, meaning they can easily tell how far objects are from each other. This is good for swooping down on mice in the dark.

Powerful Owl

Owls have a "third eyelid" called a nictitating membrane. It's translucent so the owl can see through it, and it protects the owl's eyes from injury.

An owl cannot move its eyes. Instead, it can swivel its neck almost all the way around.

Bismark wandered over to a swampy, muddy spot on the bank of a small river. A large saltwater crocodile stuck its head out of some bushes.

Bismark shrieked and scampered up a nearby tree.

"Oh, goodness!" Tobin gasped.

"Yes, maybe having some distance is not a bad idea, Bismark," Dawn said.

Chapter 8
HUGE CROCS

The saltwater crocodile, or salty, is the world's largest croc. Not only that, it's also the largest reptile on Earth. Salties can weigh over 2,000 pounds (907 kg)! Some of the biggest giants can grow as long as half the length of a bus. Equally impressive are salties' heavy, bony plates called scutes, which form a protective armor.

Saltwater Crocodile

FUN FACT
Saltwater crocodiles have specialized eyes that help them see in salt water.

Sea Swimmers

These giant reptiles are most at home in the water. They're great swimmers, and though they prefer salty swamp water, they've also been known to swim and float far out in the open sea. Salties can spend days hunting prey—fish, sea turtles, and even sharks!

We saltwater crocs have a valve at the bottom of our mouths that closes when we open our jaws underwater. This way, we don't get water down our throats when hunting.

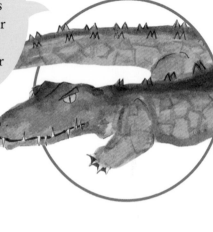

Powerful Jaws

On land, adult saltwater crocodiles prey on medium and large mammals, such as monkeys, water buffalo, and boars. The crocodile will stalk an animal—perhaps near a drinking spot by a pool or swamp—and then lunge forward and slam its jaws shut. If that's not enough, the crocodile may immediately drag the prey underwater to drown it.

DID YOU KNOW?
When baby salties are ready to hatch, they chirp to their mother.

Crocodile Moms

Female salties build nests from mud and wet grass. The mother lays about 50 eggs, which she carefully guards. She'll charge any predator that tries to come near. After the babies hatch, the mother salty carefully carries them from the nest to the water for their first swim, protecting them all the while.

Night Notes

Cold-blooded saltwater crocs can't regulate their body temperature. So, during hot Australian weather, they use shaded areas and the cool night air to keep their body temperature below 95 degrees Fahrenheit (35 degrees Celsius).

TERRIFIC TEETH

All animals have specially adapted tooth shapes that help them eat, whether they dine on plants or on other animals.

Herbivores

Plant-eating animals, such as horses and sheep which are diurnal, have flat, blocky teeth with wide surfaces. These types of teeth are good for grinding tough grasses and bark. Daylight-loving elephants have these flat teeth, too. They also have two other famous teeth, called tusks. The tusks stick out of the elephant's mouth on either side of its trunk and are handy tools for lifting, scraping, and digging.

Horse

Great White Shark

Sharks

Great white sharks—excellent hunters with periods of day and nighttime rest—have 300 teeth shaped like knives with serrated, or bumpy, edges and set in multiple rows. When sharks shed their teeth, the front teeth are lost first and the back teeth move up to take their place.

Crocodiles and Alligators

Both of these reptile cousins have sharp teeth set in jaws so powerful they can bite through tough stuff like a turtle's shell. Instead of using their teeth for chewing, though, the crocs rip their food into chunks before swallowing. When their teeth get too worn down, both crocodiles and alligators can shed their chompers and grow new ones.

American Alligator

The Nocturnals arrived in a forest in the mountains of New Zealand.

Leaves and sticks littered the ground at their feet.

"The perfect place to see a kiwi," Dawn said, looking around.

Chapter 9
KIWIS ON THE GROUND

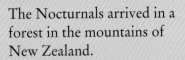

A kiwi doesn't soar above the clouds on outstretched wings. This large bird is strictly grounded and lives only in New Zealand. Kiwis strut through the forests on long, strong legs and feet, but their wings are tiny.

Kiwis are a part of a group of flightless birds called ratites. Ostriches and emus are also in this club. Though you might have to look twice at a kiwi.

Kiwis are covered in feathers that are so shaggy looking it appears as if they're covered in loose brown fur. In fact, kiwis look so much like furry animals that they're sometimes called "honorary mammals"!

Kiwi

FUN FACT
The name "kiwi" is a Maori word. It refers to the sound the male bird makes when it calls.

ENORMOUS EGG
A female kiwi lays unusually large eggs for her size. If a chicken laid an egg that large, the egg would be the size of an apple!

That's a Big Egg!

When it's time to make a nest, kiwis dig burrows in the ground, with one entrance and a room big enough for two—a male and a female.

Kiwi babies feed on the giant egg yolk while in the shell. When they hatch, they have all their feathers like adult kiwis. After just one week, they're strong enough to find their own food, so their parents don't need to help them.

We keep track of our partners by calling out as we search separately for food. Some people say that when us females call out, we sound like an old door creaking open!

Super Sniffers

About two feet tall (60 cm), the kiwi trots on short, strong legs. It snuffles along the ground, using its sharp nostrils to help it sniff out insects, worms, and fungi on the forest floor. Once it finds a tasty morsel, the kiwi pulls it out of the ground with its long, sensitive beak.

Night Notes

Unlike owls, the nocturnal kiwi can't rely on its eyesight to help it get around at night. Instead, it uses its sharp hearing and sense of smell to find its way through the dark landscape. In fact, a kiwi is the only bird on Earth that has nostrils near the tip of its beak!

"Whoa, is that rock moving over there?" Bismark said, leaning in closer to investigate.

"Hmm," Tobin said. "It is gray. But it's also a little scaly. I don't think it's a rock."

"It's a tuatara!" Dawn said. "Hello, we are The Nocturnals."

Tuatara

DON'T RUSH THE TUATARA!

Scientists call the tuatara a "living fossil." That's because this cold-blooded creature is the last of a type of reptile that has been around since the dinosaurs. All of the others in this group died out about 60 million years ago. Tuataras can live a long time—sometimes over 100 years! In fact, scientists don't know exactly how long a tuatara can live. The animals that have been studied the longest are still alive!

FUN FACT
The spiny reptile is beloved in New Zealand and has shown up on coins and postage stamps.

We get our name from the Maori word for "peaks on the back." We can raise and lower our back spines, so they are either lying flat or sticking straight up!

New Zealand Native

Tuataras aren't big travelers. They live only in New Zealand, and one species lives only on one particular island in the Cook Strait. Tuataras like to make their homes near the sea, in scrubby forest areas. They especially like loose, sandy soil so they can dig shallow burrows for shelter and protection.

Amazing Eyes

Tuataras have fantastic night vision, which helps them hunt in the dark. They can even focus each eye independently of one another. Though this reptile doesn't stop

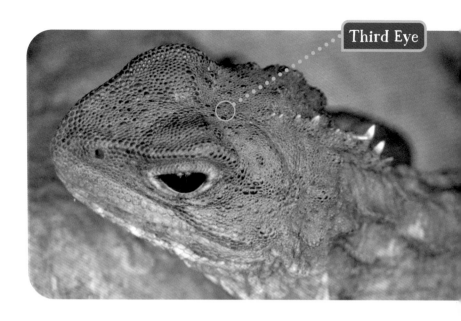

Third Eye

with two eyes. The tuatara has a "third eye" on top of its head! The eye has all the same parts, including a retina, lens, and nerves; however, it's not for seeing. Instead, it is covered with scales. It helps the tuatara sense light, absorb the sun's rays, and even regulate its body to the changing seasons.

Night Notes

While some animals like warm temperatures, tuataras prefer cooler ones. Though sometimes they'll lie in the sun during the day, most tuataras keep cool by hunting at night when the sun goes down.

Coming Out of the Egg

Females only lay eggs between every two and five years. Then, the babies grow inside the eggs for over a year. The mother doesn't stick around to meet her babies, though. She leaves the eggs before they're hatched. That means the baby tuataras have to quickly dig holes before they get snatched up by predators.

TAIL DEFENSE
A tuatara can regrow its tail if the tail gets bitten off by a predator.

DID YOU KNOW?
The oldest known tuatara is 118 years old.

Threats to Tuataras

Tuataras have faced challenges for many years. In response, the government has started several conservation programs to protect tuataras and their habitats. The programs are helping, but tuataras face yet another challenge: climate change. Tuatara babies develop inside their eggs as male or female, depending on the temperature outside. Warmer temperatures turn the babies male. Now, with rising global temperatures, more and more tuataras are born as males. If too many males are born, there won't be enough females to breed.

The Madagascar jungle was alive with chirping and buzzing sounds as The Nocturnals landed. Suddenly, an animal appeared, tapping a branch with a long middle finger.

"An aye-aye!" Bismark hollered and scampered up the trunk. "Well hello there, fellow!"

Aye-Aye

Chapter 11
LONG-FINGERED AYE-AYES

The aye-aye, the world's largest nocturnal primate, can look scary. In Madagascar, they're sometimes thought of as an omen of bad luck. Yet these tree-loving lemurs have amazing features, including fantastic eyesight and hearing. They can even hear larvae and grubs moving inside a tree branch!

FUN FACT
Aye-ayes can dangle from tree branches using their opposable big toes.

When we feel threatened, we can puff up our fur, making ourselves look almost twice as big.

The aye-aye uses an extra-long middle finger to tap tree branches. With its huge ears, it uses *echolocation* to listen for sounds that tell it an insect tunnel is inside. It is also the only primate to hunt with echolocation— the same system many bats use to navigate in the dark.

The aye-aye bites into the wood with its strong teeth until it reaches the tunnel. Then, it digs the larvae out with the long middle finger. Delicious!

FANTASTIC FUR
The aye-aye's dark fur helps it blend in with its nighttime habitat.

After a long night of searching for insects, they snuggle into cozy nests woven with twigs and leaves. The nests look like balls high up in the tree branches, with one little hole to climb into.

Night Notes

An aye-aye's huge eyes have a special layer at the back that reflects light, giving them super night vision.

BALANCING ACT
An aye-aye uses its long, furry tail to balance as it moves through the treetops.

Family Life

Aye-ayes only interact with other aye-ayes when they're looking for a mate or when a mother is raising her baby. Aye-ayes spend most of their lives alone even though they're good communicators.

Funny Faces

The aye-aye and other lemurs communicate with all sorts of facial expressions, just like humans do. They widen their eyes, bare their teeth, make pouty lips, and move their eyebrows up and down. They can make lots of different calls, too—from the soft purrs of an infant communicating to its mother to a "this is my territory" howl that can be heard for over half a mile (0.8 km).

DID YOU KNOW?
Aye-ayes are endangered animals, meaning they are at risk of going extinct.

ENDANGERED ANIMALS

Indian Pangolin

Aye-Aye

The aye-aye is just one of many nocturnal animals around the globe who are in trouble. The main problem for animals is that their homes are changing quickly, or even being destroyed. This is called habitat destruction, and it's a main threat to 85 percent of endangered and threatened animals.

For instance, when forests are cut down for farmland, or when people build

Woylie

Southern Hairy-Nosed Wombat

Eastern Barred Bandicoot

homes and parking lots, they also destroy the grasses, trees, and burrows in which nocturnal animals live. Climate change warms the oceans, making them too warm for some animals to survive. Areas that are dry become drier, and other spots flood. So it's important that in the fight to protect animals, we also protect their habitats.

In Mongolia, The Nocturnals gazed across the waving grasslands. "Look," Bismark said. "See how cute these jerboas are!"

Tobin giggled. "Oh, yes, they are cute!"

Dawn smiled at the hopping rodents.

Long-Eared Jerboa

Chapter 12

JUMPING JERBOAS

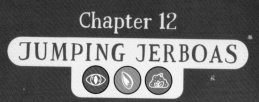

Out in the dry grasslands of Mongolia, a small creature bounds through the air. It's a jerboa! This hopping rodent not only looks adorable, it's also great at surviving in dry habitats. Thirty-three species leap through grasslands and deserts from Asia to northern Africa.

FUN FACT
A jerboa's large, round eyes let in plenty of light so it can see in the dark.

Severtzov's Jerboa

On the Move

Jerboas are great jumpers, and some can leap up to 10 feet (3 m) on their springlike back feet. Picture an animal the size of a mouse jumping far above the head of a fully grown man! Jerboas can even jump sideways to confuse predators on the prowl. Stiff tufts of hair on the soles of jerboas' feet help them jump on slippery sand. When they're not jumping, jerboas scamper or hop to get around.

DID YOU KNOW?
A jerboa's tail can be longer than its body and helps the animal balance when jumping.

Lesser Egyptian Jerboa

Night Notes

Most jerboas have giant ears that help them hear predators at night. Their ears also help keep them cool in the hot desert by circulating and cooling off their blood and releasing heat.

Protective Burrows

This little rodent knows how to protect itself against predators in its desert home. It's a powerful digger and builds two different kinds of burrows: one for sleeping during the day and one for quick shelter while foraging for food at night. Some species build a permanent burrow to hibernate in during the winter. Other species in hot deserts will hibernate during the summer months.

NO WATER NEEDED
Jerboas get almost all the water they need from the food they eat. In fact, a jerboa might not drink water at all during its lifetime!

Four-Toed Jerboa

Lesser Egyptian Jerboa

FUN FACT
A jerboa's fur usually grows to match the color of its desert habitat.

To keep out the hot desert air and maintain cool temperatures and moisture, some jerboas plug the hole of their burrows with dirt and sand.

Jerboa Babies

Jerboa babies are born without fur and with small hind feet. Their feet don't grow to their full, long size until the jerboa is about eight weeks old. Then, over the course of several weeks, the baby jerboa must learn to jump.

BRINGING UP BABY

Baby jerboas, like many nocturnal baby animals, need lots of attention and care before they can head out on their own. Here are some unusual ways nocturnal animals are welcomed into the world:

Bats

When a mother bat gives birth, she does so while hanging upside down! And mom has to move fast—once the baby, called a pup, emerges, mom quickly catches the newborn in her wings. A baby bat often takes a ride with mom on her nighttime flights.

Flying Fox

Echidna

Monotremes

Nocturnal echidnas and platypuses are types of egg-laying mammals that are also called monotremes. Monotreme babies use a special kind of tooth called a "milk tooth" to hatch from small, leathery eggs. Then their mothers feed the babies milk until they're ready to find their own food at about 20 weeks old.

Marsupials

Quokka

These mammals raise their babies in pouches. The babies are usually only about the size of a jelly bean. So they finish developing inside mom's pouch. This process takes several months. Some marsupials, such as kangaroos, are not ready to explore outside of the pouch until they're about six months old.

Red Kangaroo

In a dense, swampy jungle, snakes hung from the trees and slithered through the underbrush.

"You know, friends, I really prefer to meet vipers from a distance," Bismark said.

Chapter 13

VENOMOUS VIPERS

The mangrove pit viper, which is also called the shore pit viper, is part of a large group of snakes. Vipers are found all over the world—from Europe and North America to Asia and South America—and all species are venomous; however, the amount of *venom* a viper might have is different based on where

Mangrove Pit Viper

FUN FACT
Copperheads and rattlesnakes are well-known members of the pit viper family.

it lives. Viper species in colder northern climates have less venom than those in hotter, more southern climates.

No matter where they live, vipers can be sneaky hunters. They hold still and move slowly—that is, until they see something delicious. Then, they strike fast, sometimes in less than one second.

I have a pit between each eye and nostril that help me sense heat given off by my prey—all the better to strike fast.

Fearsome Fangs

A viper has large, curved fangs that are hollow. Venom is stored inside glands behind the viper's eyes. When the viper bites prey, the venom travels down from the glands into the fangs—and then into the unlucky victim. When the viper is not attacking prey, the fangs fold neatly up inside the snake's mouth.

Powerful Hunters

When a viper does use its venom, it has to wait until its body can make more. So vipers conserve their venom carefully. Some vipers

STRONG SCALES
Most vipers have keeled scales. This means that instead of being smooth, there's a ridge that runs on each one, making them feel rough.

bite their prey and immediately let go. This is so the wounded animal can't bite or attack back. The prey runs off and eventually dies from the venom. Then, the viper sniffs out the dead prey and often eats it whole.

Night Notes

Most snakes are active during the day, when they can use the sun to help regulate their body temperature. However, the mangrove pit viper hunts under the cover of darkness.

In New Mexico, The Nocturnals spotted a mother coyote and her pups trotting through the scrubby grasses.

"Hello," Dawn called out.

She scampered over to them, with Tobin and Bismark close behind.

"We are so glad to see you awake at night. We weren't sure if you'd be sleeping or not."

Coyote

Chapter 14

CLEVER COYOTES

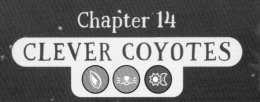

Is that a coyote hunting in a desert? Yes. Is that a coyote stalking a chicken coop on a farm? Yes! Is that a coyote living in some shrubs in a city neighborhood? Yes, it is!

This versatile animal can live in almost any habitat, eat pretty much any food, live near people or away from people, and hunt alone or in groups. In fact, most cities in the United States are home to coyotes. Often, people in those cities have no idea coyotes are living near them!

FUN FACT
Coyotes are fast—they can run up to 40 miles an hour (64 km/h).

We coyotes aren't picky eaters. We'll eat anything from rodents to snakes— even rotting meat!

Comparing Canids

Because coyotes look like small wolves and often live in grasslands, some people call them "prairie wolves." They're not wolves, though they are relatives. Coyotes are *canids*, just like dogs, wolves, and foxes.

Smart Hunters

Coyotes can live alone, but they generally move in packs made up of a male-female leader pair and others, who are usually relatives. They hunt alone or in pairs, unlike wolves, who both live in packs and

hunt in packs. If hunting is scarce in the fall and winter, coyotes will hunt in packs. They'll chase down a deer until it falls from exhaustion, or they will drive the deer toward other waiting pack members.

COYOTE CALLS

Coyotes sometimes howl in packs, and when in distress, a coyote's call can sound like a human screaming or shouting.

PUPS GROW UP
Coyote babies are born in the spring and start hunting on their own by the fall.

Coyote Bedtime

No cozy nests for coyotes! These canids like to bed down in the open, except when it's time to have babies. Mother coyotes will build one or more dens for her pups. She might use an old raccoon burrow, or she might scratch out a hole herself under bushes. She might even crawl into an old, hollow tree to find a safe place to give birth. She'll often move her pups to a different den several times. That way, predators like eagles, bears, and wolves will have a harder time sniffing out the pups.

Playful Pups

Once the babies are born, the whole coyote pack takes care of them. The mother nurses the babies, and the father and other pack members hunt for her and watch over the babies when she is hunting for herself.

Once the babies are older, they start exploring outside the den and the whole pack babysits to keep the pups safe from predators.

Night Notes

Depending on where coyotes live, they might be nocturnal...or not! In areas with lots of people, coyotes sleep during the day and hunt at night, dawn, or dusk to avoid human contact. In places without humans, coyotes tend to be awake during the day.

"Bismark?" Dawn called out. Where did he go?

Dawn and Tobin padded toward the forest and then heard Bismark shouting.

"Dawn! Tooobinn! Look what I've found— flying friends!"

Chapter 15

NIGHT-FLYING BATS

In a dark cave, thousands of tiny bats hang upside down, clustered together. They're sleeping with their wings wrapped around them. When the sun sets and darkness falls, they awaken and burst out of the cave opening, fluttering into the sky. Before the night is over, the bats will catch thousands of insects—almost their entire

Greater Horseshoe Bat

FUN FACT
Bat poop, also called guano, is a prized fertilizer and rich in nutrients that are good for the soil.

Not all bats eat bugs. Some large bats in the tropics eat fruit or even fish. The famous vampire bats drink blood from cattle, horses, and other large mammals; however, they're not bloodsuckers. Vampire bats make a small cut in the animal's skin with their sharp teeth. Then, they lap up the blood that seeps out.

The Nose Knows

Found in parts of Africa, Asia, and Europe, the greater horseshoe bat has a fleshy nose shaped like...well, a horseshoe. This nose leaf actually helps the bat navigate. It collects sound waves that the bat uses to guide itself—much like a human ear guides sound into the ear canal. The greater horseshoe bat also makes sounds through its nose rather than its mouth. These noises help guide the bat as it swoops and dives.

Fly, Baby, Fly!

A baby bat is born without hair and is unable to fly. Its first weeks of life are spent in the nest with its mother. It even rides along with her as she flies through the night. As the baby bat grows bigger and stronger, the mother starts encouraging it to fly. She nudges the baby so that it flaps around. Gradually, it starts learning that it can fly, too!

Night Notes

Most bats use something called echolocation to find their way around. They make twittering noises, which bounce off nearby objects like trees or other animals. Most of these sounds are outside the range of human hearing.

Some of us bats can grow big! The largest bat on Earth is the flying fox. It has wings that stretch out as wide as an adult is tall!

ALL ABOUT ECHOLOCATION

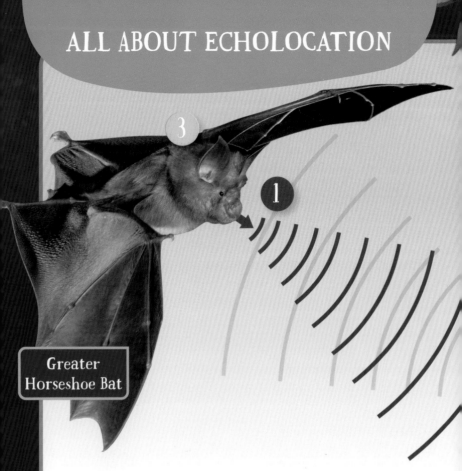

Greater Horseshoe Bat

Imagine "seeing" the world using only sound waves! That's exactly how bats and some other animals navigate. All of these calculations happen in a split second. In the dark, bats can sense an object as thin as a hair and as tiny as a mosquito.

Bats aren't the only mammals that move through the world using sound senses—dolphins and whales use echolocation, too.

1 Bats send out sound using their noses or mouths.

2 The sound waves bounce off objects and send back echoes.

3 Bats listen to the echoes, and their brains are able to interpret what is around them.

Mexican Free-Tailed Bats

Even some people who are visually impaired use echolocation! Just as bats do, these people have learned to make rapid clicking noises and listen to the sounds to help "see" the objects around them.

The Nocturnals
adventure has come
to an end...

...for now.

"What was your favorite animal?" Tobin asked his friends as he snuffled his snout at a nearby termite mound. "I liked the kiwi. She gets mistaken for a mammal, just like I get mistaken for a reptile," Tobin explained.

"The aye-aye caught my eye!" Bismark said, winking. "A long finger like that would come in handy for many things—not just scooping out flower pollen!"

Dawn listened as her rust colored fur glittered in the moonlight. "I don't think I can choose a favorite. Each nocturnal animal is unique and fascinating."

"You're right, Dawn," Tobin said. "A tuatara has an eye on the top of its head. Crocodiles can grow new teeth. Sugar gliders like Bismark can soar from the tallest treetops!"

"Indeed I can, my pangolin pal!" Bismark said and glided down from his tree branch.

Dawn smiled at her friends. "We are all special."

As the moon set and the eastern sky lightened with the dawn, it was time for The Nocturnals to go home. Their travels were over. Now it was time to go to sleep.

NOCTURNAL ANIMAL GLOSSARY

AYE-AYE

Scientific Name: *Daubentonia madagascariensis*
Physical Characteristics: mammal; 12 inches (31 cm) long; large, round eyes; excellent night vision; distinctive long middle finger on its front paws
Behavioral Characteristics: nocturnal, uses its long finger to tap tree branches and trunks to locate larvae, solitary, spends almost all its life in trees
Diet: wood larvae, fruit, nuts
Habitat: Madagascar, forest
Status: endangered

BANDICOOT

Scientific Name: *Peramelemorphia*
Physical Characteristics: mammal; anywhere from 12 to 31 inches (31 to 79 cm) long; strong, pointed snout; powerful, curved front paws; marsupial with backward-facing front pouch; excellent sense of smell
Behavioral Characteristics: nocturnal, solitary, digs up a wide variety of foods with its strong snout
Diet: roots, insects, fruit, larvae, snails, mice, seeds
Habitat: Australia, brushy areas
Status: mixed; six species are stable, five are vulnerable, two are endangered, and one is extinct

THE NOCTURNALS

COYOTE

Scientific Name: *Canis latrans*

Physical Characteristics: mammal, 3 to 4 feet (1 to 1.2 m) long, small canid, gray or brown fur, pointed snout, upstanding ears, bushy tail, excellent sense of hearing and smell

Behavioral Characteristics: nocturnal, diurnal, or crepuscular depending on habitat; hunts alone or in packs; cares for the young in groups; adaptable to a wide range of habitats and food sources

Diet: small mammals, frogs, fish, berries, carrion, garbage if need be

Habitat: North America, grasslands, desert, mountains, urban areas

Status: stable

GREATER HORSESHOE BAT

Scientific Name: *Rhinolophus ferrumequinum*

Physical Characteristics: mammal, from 2 to 3 inches (50 to 76 mm) long, nose leaf helps direct sound waves toward ears, skin-and-bone wings, uses echolocation to hunt and navigate

Behavioral Characteristics: nocturnal, fast flyer, swift glider and diver

Diet: insects

Habitat: Europe, northern Africa, Asia, grasslands, forests

Status: stable

JERBOA

Scientific Name: 33 species under the family Dipodidae

Physical Characteristics: mammal; 2 to 5 inches (5 to 13 cm) long; large, strong back feet; short front limbs; some species with large ears; big eyes; hair on bottoms of paws

Behavioral Characteristics: nocturnal, jumps up to six feet (2 m) to hunt and avoid predators, builds different types of burrows in sand or soil

Diet: insects, seeds, roots

Habitat: China, Mongolia, grasslands, deserts

Status: some populations are stable, while others are near-threatened

KIWI

Scientific Name: five species under the genus *Apteryx*

Physical Characteristics: bird; between 18 and 21 inches (45 to 54 cm) long; flightless; spends life on the ground; shaggy, fine brown feathers; lays large eggs; nostrils near the tip of beak

Behavioral Characteristics: nocturnal, uses scent and hearing to find food, fast runner, digs burrows for nesting

Diet: earthworms

Habitat: New Zealand, brushy areas, forests

Status: some populations are stable, while others are near-threatened

THE NOCTURNALS

MANGROVE PIT VIPER

Scientific Name: *Trimeresurus purpureomaculatus*
Physical Characteristics: reptile, between 1 and
2 feet (0.3 to 0.6 m) long, hollow fangs, often
injects venom when biting
Behavioral Characteristics: nocturnal, stalks prey and then
strikes quickly, bites prey and then releases
Diet: rodents, frogs, lizards, birds
Habitat: Thailand, swamps, wet forests
Status: stable

PANGOLIN

Scientific Name: eight species under the
order Pholidota
Physical Characteristics: mammal; between 1 and
4 feet (0.3 to 1.2 m) long; covered in scales; long,
sticky tongue; strong, curved front claws
Behavioral Characteristics: nocturnal, digs into ant and
termite mounds for food, licks up insects with its long
tongue, digs burrows
Diet: ants, termites, insects
Habitat: Africa, Asia, grasslands, deserts, forests
Status: some populations are vulnerable, endangered, and
critically endangered

POWERFUL OWL

Scientific Name: *Ninox strenua*
Physical Characteristics: bird, wings up to 4.5 feet (1.4 m) across, largest owl in Australia, excellent eyesight and hearing, facial disk of stiff feathers helps direct sound, fixed binocular vision, neck rotates almost 360 degrees
Behavioral Characteristics: nocturnal, roosts in trees during the day, hunts at night
Diet: possums, large bats, rabbits
Habitat: Australia, grasslands, wooded areas
Status: stable

SALTWATER CROCODILE

Scientific Name: *Crocodylus porosus*
Physical Characteristics: reptile, 17 feet (5 m) long, grows up to 1,000 pounds (454 kg), excellent swimmer, specialized eyes to see under water, develops multiple sets of teeth over its lifetime, can use only one brain hemisphere at a time
Behavioral Characteristics: nocturnal (though will sometimes hunt during the day), aggressive hunter, swims out to sea to hunt, waits for prey near water
Diet: large and small mammals and large fish, including monkeys, water buffalo, boars, sharks
Habitat: India, Southeast Asia, Australia, brackish swamps
Status: stable

SUGAR GLIDER

Scientific Name: *Petaurus breviceps*
Physical Characteristics: mammal, about 5 to 6 inches (13 to 15 cm) long, flaps of skin connect front and back limbs, large eyes and ears, excellent night vision
Behavioral Characteristics: nocturnal, social, lives in large colonies, glides from tree to tree using skin flaps, spends life in treetops
Diet: tree sap, pollen, insects, small birds
Habitat: Australia, Papua New Guinea, Indonesia, wooded areas
Status: stable

RED FOX

Scientific Name: *Vulpes vulpes*
Physical Characteristics: mammal, about 3 feet (0.9 m) long, bushy tail with white tip, excellent hearing and sense of smell
Behavioral Characteristics: nocturnal, diurnal, or crepuscular depending on habitat; uses listen and leap technique for catching prey; fast runner; solitary; adaptable, can live in a wide variety of habitats and environments
Diet: rabbits, rodents, fish, berries, roots, fruit, carrion, garbage if need be
Habitat: worldwide, deserts, mountains, forests, grasslands
Status: stable

TUATARA

Scientific Name: *Sphenodon punctatus*
Physical Characteristics: reptile; between 1 and 3 feet (0.3 to 0.9 m) long; can focus eyes independently of each other; third eye on top of its head for sensing light; long-lived, up to 100 years; good night vision
Behavioral Characteristics: nocturnal (though sometimes basks in the sun during the day), slow-moving, lives alone, young hunt at night to avoid being eaten by older tuataras
Diet: smaller lizards, birds, rodents
Habitat: New Zealand, scrubby areas
Status: stable due to New Zealand conservation management efforts

WOMBAT

Scientific Name: Vombatidae
Physical Characteristics: mammal; between 2 and 4 feet (0.6 to 1.2 m) long; constantly grows front teeth; tough bottoms armored with fat and cartilage; clumsy, waddling walk; fast runner
Behavioral Characteristics: nocturnal, digs burrows for sleeping, gnaws wood to trim down teeth, marks eating areas with distinct scent
Diet: grasses, tree bark
Habitat: Australia, grassy, wooded areas
Status: mixed: some species are stable, some are near-threatened, and one is critically endangered

WOYLIE

Scientific Name: *Bettongia penicillata*
Physical Characteristics: mammal, about 1 foot
(0.3 m) long, stands upright, long hind feet,
strong front paws, prehensile tail
Behavioral Characteristics: nocturnal, constantly digs in
search of food, good sense of smell, carries bedding in tail,
fights by lying on side and kicking feet
Diet: fungi
Habitat: Australia, shrubby areas
Status: critically endangered

Learn more about endangered animals from the
IUCN Red List of Threatened Species

iucnredlist.org

All of the animals featured in this book appear in
The Nocturnals book series by Tracey Hecht:

- *The Mysterious Abductions*
- *The Ominous Eye*
- *The Hidden Kingdom*
- *The Fallen Star*

WORD GLOSSARY

Adaptation—a change in which an animal becomes better suited to its environment

Cache—a collection of objects like food, hidden in a secret place

Canid—a member of the dog family

Cathemeral—active at irregular times

Climate—the weather in a certain area over a long period of time

Crepuscular—active during dawn and dusk

Diurnal—active during the day

Echolocation—the location of objects using reflected sound waves

Keratin—a type of protein that makes up hair, feathers, scales, nails, claws, hooves, and horns

Nocturnal—active at night

Omnivore—an animal that eats both meat and plants

Predator—an animal that eats other animals

Prehensile—capable of grasping, especially with a tail

Prey—an animal that is eaten by other animals

Species—a group of animals who can have babies together and share genes

Venom—a poison secreted by animals and injected by biting or stinging

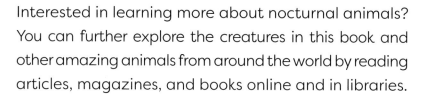

RESEARCH TIPS

Interested in learning more about nocturnal animals? You can further explore the creatures in this book and other amazing animals from around the world by reading articles, magazines, and books online and in libraries.

- **Always use reliable sources** when you're doing research for school—or even just for yourself! The websites of organizations, museums, zoos, and government agencies are great places to look for reliable facts. Reputable online magazines and news organizations are also excellent sources of information. Their websites have usually been fact-checked by experts.

- **Videos online can also be a great resource** for research. Ask a grown-up to help you find documentaries from public television stations, zoos, conservation organizations, and museums. Practice taking notes while you watch.

- **Practice your journalism skills** by interviewing an expert! Local zoos and universities are packed with experts who can provide interesting, fact-based information. Start by making a list of questions you'd like to ask an expert. With an adult's help, search online for an email address and then email that person with your name, why you'd like to interview them, and the general topic and questions you'd like to discuss.

- **Be sure to cite your sources.** If you don't know how, just note the website address for each fact you use. Then, later, you can ask a teacher or a parent how to correctly cite the source. If you quote a source directly—use exactly the same words the source uses—always place those words in quotation marks and add the website address where you found it.

INDEX

Grey Long-Eared Bat

Jerboa

Powerful Owl

Sugar Glider

About the Author

Tracey Hecht is a writer and entrepreneur who has written, directed, and produced for film. She created a Nocturnals Read Aloud Writing Program in partnership with the New York Public Library that has expanded nationwide. Tracey splits her time between Oquossoc, Maine, and New York City with her husband and four children.

About the Science Writer

Emma Carlson Berne is a children's book author. She often writes about plants, animals, and the natural world. Emma lives in Cincinnati, Ohio, with her husband and three boys.

About Fabled Films & Fabled Films Press

Fabled Films is a publishing and entertainment company that creates original content for young readers and middle-grade audiences. Fabled Films Press combines strong literary properties with high-quality production values to connect books with generations of parents and their children. The book program was developed under the supervision of science educators and reading specialists to develop kids' reading skills and support national science standards. Each property is supported by websites, educator guides, and activities for bookstores, educators, and librarians, as well as videos, social media content, and supplemental entertainment for additional platforms.

FABLED FILMS PRESS
NEW YORK CITY

Connect with Fabled Films and The Nocturnals:
www.NocturnalsWorld.com | www.fabledfilms.com
 Facebook | Instagram: @NocturnalsWorld
 Twitter: @fabled_films

Photo Credits

Front Cover: sugar glider, Kurit afshen/Shutterstock; fox, Jim Cumming/Shutterstock; pangolin, Fabian von Poser/imageBROKER RF/Getty Images; **Back Cover:** aye-aye, Thorsten Negro/imageBROKER/Age Fotostock; tuatara, Mark Walshe/Shutterstock.

Top=t, Center=c, Bottom=b, Left=l, Right=r, Shutterstock=Sh

Photos: 5, dangdumrong/Sh; 8, Vaclav Matous/Sh; 9le, BeautifulPicture/Sh; 9rt, Pedro Ferreira do Amaral/Getty/iStock; 10t, Seregraff/Getty/iStock; 10c, Geza Farkas/Sh; 10b, Michal Ninger/Sh; 11t, Jennifer McCallum/Sh; 11c, Ondrej Prosicky/Sh; 11b, Positive Snapshot/Sh; 12-13 fox, Menno Schaefer/Sh; 12-13 grass, Sanit Fuangnakhon/Sh; 14, Stanislav Duben/Sh; 15, Anolis01/Getty/iStock; 16t, DamianKuzdak/E+/Getty Images; 16c, Giedriius/Sh; 16b, Szczepan Klejbuk/Sh; 18, Richard Seeley/Sh; 19, Giedriius/Sh; 20-21 alt, Neal Herbert/NPS; 21, Hanna Knutsson/Sh; 22-23, Jiri Prochazka/Adobe Stock; 24, Vicky Chauhan/Getty/iStock; 26, 2630ben/Getty/iStock; 27, Angiolo/Adobe Stock; 28-29, Fourleaflover/Getty/iStock; 28l, David Pineda Svenske/Sh; 28tr, Angiolo/Adobe Stock; 28br, hphimagelibrary/Getty/iStock; 29tl, Positive Snapshot/Sh; 29tr, Khlongwangchao/Getty/iStock; 29br, Binturong-tonoscarpe/Sh; 30-31, Arif Supriyadi/Sh; 32, Anom Harya/Sh; 33, Ari wibowo/Getty/iStock; 34, Frank Yuwono/Age Fotostock; 35, Wayan Sumatika/Sh; 36, LKR Photography/Getty/iStock; 37, Kamonrat/Sh; 38, Potray/Sh; 39t, Cede Prudente/Getty/iStock; 39b, Agami Photo Agency/Sh; 40, Sonijya/Sh; 41, Jonas Boernicke/Sh; 42, Andreas Ruhz/Sh; 43, Pixelheld/Sh; 44, 45, Susan Flashman/Sh; 46, animalinfo/Getty/iStock; 47, Albert Wright/Getty/iStock; 48, Luke Shelley/Sh; 49, fotofritz16/Getty/iStock; 50l, Megan Griffin/Sh; 50t, Stuart Elflett/Sh; 51l, Fourleaflover/Getty/iStock; 51r, Carla Thomas/Sh; 52, Michal Sloviak/Sh; 53, Lukas Blazek/Dreamstime; 54, mb-fotos/Getty/iStock; 56, Ken Griffiths/Sh; 57, Trevor Scouten/Sh; 58, Luke Shelley/Sh; 59, Ken Griffiths/Sh; 60, colin robert varndell/Sh; 61t, Ken Griffiths/Sh; 61b, Susan Flashman/Sh; 62, Firepac/Sh; 63, Reinhard Dirscherl/The Image Bank RF/Getty Images; 64, chameleonseye/Getty/iStock; 65, Supermop/Sh; 66-67 teeth, Eric Isselee/Sh; 66l, Studio 37/Sh; 67t, Sergey Uryadnikov/Sh; 67c, Mia2you/Sh; 68, Smithsonian Institution; 69, Vee Snijders/Sh; 70, chameleonseye/Getty/iStock; 71, Allan Pritchard/Sh; 72-73, Ross Gordon Henry/Sh; 73b, Manakin/Getty/iStock; 74, Alizada Studios/Sh; 75, Anna Dunlop/Sh; 76, Lisa Crawford/Sh; 77, HannaTor/Sh; 78-79 aye-aye, Dale McDonald/Adobe Stock; 78-79 grass, Kriengsuk Prasroetsung/Sh; 80, Eugen Haag/Sh; 81, Coulanges/Sh; 82, dennisvdw/Getty/iStock; 83, Thorsten Negro/imageBROKER/Age Fotostock; 84-85 deforestation, jax10289/Getty/iStock; 84t, Positive Snapshot/Sh; 84c, Rinus Baak/Dreamstime; 85t, slowmotiongli/Sh; 85bl, Susan Flashman/Sh; 85r, Henry Cook/Moment Open/Getty; 86-87 jerboa, Lauren Suryanata/Sh; 86-87 rocks, Somchai Boonpun/Sh; 88, edmon/Sh; 89, Konrad Wothe/imageBROKER/Agefotostock; 90, Yerbolat Shadrakhov/Sh; 91, weisschr/Getty/iStock; 92, Nico Faramaz/Sh; 93t, almondd/Sh; 93cl, EA Given/Sh; 93r, Brayden Stanford/Getty/iStock; 94, Lauren Suryanata/Sh; 95, Dicky Asmoro/Sh; 96, shinji nakano/Sh; 97, Andrew M West/Sh; 98-99 coyote, Warren Metcalf/Sh; 98-99 rocks, Kamonrat/Sh; 101t, Chris/Adobe Stock; 101b, Warren Metcalf/Sh; 102, Chris/Adobe Stock; 103, Danita Delimont/Sh; 104, Carl Allen/Sh; 105, aaltair/Sh; 106, Real PIX/Sh; 108, 109t, Carl Allen/Sh; 109l, Rob Lavers RIBA ARPS/Sh; 109r, Ann Froschauer/USFWS; 112t, Eugen Haag/Sh; 112b, Stanley Teixeira/Dreamstime; 113t, Tom Koerner/USFWS; 113b, Real PIX/Sh; 114t, Greens and Blues/Sh; 114b, Lakeview Images/Sh; 115t, Vladimir Turkenich/Sh; 115b, Mike Gordon/Sh; 116t, Trevor Scouten/Sh; 116b, dangdumrong/Sh; 117t, Mark Bridger/Sh; 117b, Rejean Bedard/Sh; 118t, Tal Haim/Adobe Stock; 118b, 3sby/Sh; 119, slowmotiongli/Getty/iStock; 122, Geza Farkas/Sh; 123, edmon/Sh; 124, Trevor Scouten/Sh; 125, Anom Harya/Sh.

All of The Nocturnals artwork is courtesy of Fabled Films, LLC.

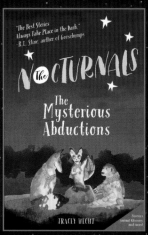
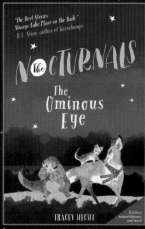